GLUCOSE GODDESS
Method Recipe Cookbook

Empowering Your Health and Vitality through Diet and Blood Sugar Management

Dr. Maryann D. Clerke

Copyright © 2023 **Dr. Maryann D. Clerke**

All Rights reserved. No piece of this book might be duplicated or communicated in any structure or using any and all means, electronic or mechanical, including copying, recording, or by any data stockpiling and recovery framework, without consent recorded as a hard copy

TABLE OF CONTENTS

CHAPTER 1 6

    INTRODUCTION TO GLUCOSE AND HEALTH: 6

CHAPTER 2: 11

    UNDERSTANDING GLUCOSE METABOLISM 11

CHAPTER 3 18

    THE LINK BETWEEN GLUCOSE AND HEALTH CHALLENGES 18

CHAPTER 4 24

    ASSESSING YOUR GLUCOSE HEALTH 24

CHAPTER 5 30

    THE GLUCOSE GODDESS DIET PRINCIPLES 30

CHAPTER 6 36

    BUILDING A GLUCOSE-FRIENDLY PANTRY 36

CHAPTER 7 43
MEAL PLANNING FOR GLUCOSE HEALTH 43

CHAPTER 8 50
GLUCOSE GODDESS DIET RECIPES 50

BONUS CHAPTER 58

CHAPTER 9 68
MANAGING CRAVINGS AND EMOTIONAL EATING 68

CHAPTER 10 77
EXERCISE AND GLUCOSE HEALTH 77

CHAPTER 11 87
LIFESTYLE FACTORS AND GLUCOSE HEALTH 87

CHAPTER 12 94
MONITORING AND TRACKING PROGRESS................94

CHAPTER 13 104

SPECIAL CONSIDERATIONS: 104

CHAPTER 14 113

SEEKING PROFESSIONAL GUIDANCE: 113

CHAPTER 15 122

MAINTAINING LONG-TERM GLUCOSE HEALTH: 122

Chapter 1

Introduction to Glucose and Health:

Glucose, sometimes referred to as blood sugar, is a critical source of energy for the body. It serves a key role in sustaining numerous biological functions and promoting general health and well-being. In this article, we will discuss the importance of glucose, its impact on the body, and present practical answers and assistance to solve health concerns connected to glucose regulation.

UNDERSTANDING GLUCOSE: Glucose is a type of sugar that is derived from the meals we consume, mainly carbs. When we ingest carbs, they are broken down into glucose during digestion, which is subsequently taken into the bloodstream. From there, glucose is delivered to cells throughout the body to supply energy for numerous metabolic activities.

IMPORTANCE OF GLUCOSE: Glucose serves as the principal source of energy for the brain, muscles, and other physiological tissues. It fuels critical tasks such as thinking, physical activity, and the maintenance of body temperature. Without sufficient glucose, these processes can be disrupted, leading to weariness, poor cognitive function, and other health concerns.

GLUCOSE AND INSULIN: Insulin, a hormone generated by the pancreas, plays a key function in regulating glucose levels in the bloodstream. When blood glucose levels rise after a meal, insulin is released, allowing glucose to enter cells for energy usage. Insulin also helps store extra glucose in the liver and muscles for later use.

IMPACT OF GLUCOSE IMBALANCE ON HEALTH: Maintaining regulated blood glucose levels is vital for overall health. Imbalances in glucose levels can have a substantial impact on general well-being and may lead to numerous health concerns. Let's investigate some of these difficulties and their potential solutions:

DIABETES: Diabetes is a chronic disorder characterized by increased blood glucose levels. Type 1 diabetes happens when the body doesn't create enough insulin, while type 2 diabetes arises when the body becomes resistant to the effects of insulin. Both types can result in high blood glucose levels, which, if left untreated, can lead to consequences such as cardiovascular disease, renal damage, and nerve damage. Managing diabetes needs a combination of medicine, lifestyle adjustments, and regular monitoring of blood glucose levels.

HYPOGLYCEMIA: On the other end of the spectrum, hypoglycemia refers to low blood glucose levels. It can occur in patients with diabetes who use insulin or certain medicines.

Symptoms of hypoglycemia include dizziness, disorientation, perspiration, and weakness. Consuming a modest amount of glucose-rich food, such as fruit juice or glucose tablets, can immediately raise blood glucose levels and reduce symptoms.

METABOLIC SYNDROME: Metabolic syndrome is a cluster of disorders that includes high blood pressure, raised blood glucose levels, abnormal cholesterol levels, and excess belly fat. This syndrome raises the chance of developing heart disease, stroke, and type 2 diabetes. Adopting a healthy lifestyle, which includes regular physical activity, a balanced diet, and weight management, can help avoid or manage metabolic syndrome

Chapter 2:

Understanding Glucose Metabolism

In this chapter, we will investigate the intriguing process of glucose metabolism and the crucial role of insulin in regulating blood sugar levels. By offering a complete overview, we hope to increase your awareness of how your body processes glucose and offer practical answers and suggestions for enhancing your glucose health.

WHAT IS GLUCOSE METABOLISM?

Glucose metabolism is the process through which your body turns glucose, a simple sugar, into useful energy. When you consume carbohydrates, such as grains, fruits, and starchy vegetables, your body breaks them down into glucose during digestion. This glucose is subsequently carried into your circulation to be used as fuel by your cells. Through numerous metabolic pathways, glucose is digested to form ATP (adenosine triphosphate), which is the principal energy source for cellular processes.

THE ROLE OF INSULIN IN BLOOD SUGAR REGULATION

Insulin, a hormone generated by the pancreas, plays a critical function in regulating blood sugar levels. When blood glucose levels rise after a meal, the pancreas releases insulin into the bloodstream. Insulin functions as a key that unlocks the cells, allowing glucose to enter and be used for energy production. It also instructs the liver to store excess glucose as glycogen for future energy demands. By facilitating glucose uptake into cells, insulin helps lower blood sugar levels and maintain a stable glucose balance.

GLUCOSE HOMEOSTASIS: Balancing Blood Sugar Levels

Glucose homeostasis refers to the body's capacity to maintain blood sugar levels within a restricted range. It involves a complicated interaction of hormones, including insulin, glucagon, and others, to keep blood glucose in balance. When blood sugar levels are excessively high, insulin is produced to increase glucose uptake and storage. Conversely, when blood sugar levels are low, glucagon encourages the liver to release stored glucose, boosting blood sugar levels. This careful balance ensures that your body has a consistent supply of fuel while avoiding extremes in blood sugar.

GLUCOSE METABOLISM DISORDERS

Disruptions in glucose metabolism can lead to health issues. Type 1 diabetes occurs when the pancreas produces little or no insulin, resulting in elevated blood sugar levels. Type 2 diabetes, the more frequent variety, involves insulin resistance, where the body's cells do not respond properly to insulin. Gestational diabetes affects certain pregnant women, producing transient blood sugar abnormalities. Left uncontrolled, these disorders can lead to consequences, including cardiovascular disease, nerve damage, and kidney problems. Managing glucose metabolism disorders frequently involves a combination of medication, lifestyle alterations, and dietary changes.

OPTIMIZING GLUCOSE METABOLISM THROUGH DIET

Diet has a critical role in promoting appropriate glucose metabolism. By making conscious meal choices, you can assist maintain stable blood sugar levels. Focus on consuming complex carbohydrates, such as whole grains, fruits, and vegetables, as they deliver a slow and constant release of glucose. Include lean proteins, such as poultry, fish, lentils, and tofu, to improve satiety and stabilize blood sugar. Incorporate healthy fats from sources like avocados, almonds, and olive oil, as they slow down digestion and avoid blood sugar spikes. Fiber-rich foods, like beans, lentils, and vegetables, can aid to stable blood sugar levels. Portion control, regular mealtimes, and avoiding sugary beverages and processed foods are further techniques for optimizing glucose metabolism.

PHYSICAL ACTIVITY AND GLUCOSE METABOLISM

Regular physical activity has several benefits for glucose metabolism. Exercise boosts insulin sensitivity, allowing cells to take up glucose more efficiently. This helps reduce blood sugar levels and promotes overall metabolic health. Engaging in cardiovascular workouts, such as vigorous walking, jogging, or cycling, can help burn extra glucose and enhance insulin activity. Strength training exercises, such lifting weights or utilizing resistance bands, build muscular growth and boost glucose uptake by cells. Additionally, adopting an active lifestyle by including movement throughout your day, such as climbing the stairs or walking instead of driving, can have a good impact on glucose metabolism.

Chapter 3

The Link between Glucose and Health Challenges

In this chapter, we will study the substantial link between glucose abnormalities and numerous health concerns. By addressing a wide range of health issues related with glucose imbalances, such as diabetes, insulin resistance, and metabolic syndrome, we will present practical answers and assistance for optimizing glucose health and preventing or managing these challenges.

UNDERSTANDING GLUCOSE IMBALANCES

Glucose imbalances arise when blood sugar levels depart from the appropriate range. Both high blood sugar (hyperglycemia) and low blood sugar (hypoglycemia) can have detrimental consequences on general health. This section will look into the origins and implications of glucose imbalances, underlining the necessity of maintaining stable blood sugar levels.

DIABETES: A Glucose-related Health Challenge

Diabetes is a chronic illness characterized by excessive blood sugar levels. We will cover the numerous varieties of diabetes, including type 1 diabetes, type 2 diabetes, and gestational diabetes, along with its causes, risk factors, and potential complications. Practical solutions for treating diabetes, such as blood sugar monitoring, medication management, and lifestyle adjustments, will be offered.

INSULIN RESISTANCE AND ITS IMPACT ON HEALTH

Insulin resistance occurs when the body's cells become less receptive to insulin, resulting in high blood sugar levels. We will address the origins and effects of insulin resistance, including its link with obesity, sedentary lifestyle, and poor food choices. Lifestyle adjustments, including regular physical activity, weight management, and adopting a balanced diet, will be stressed as crucial methods for developing insulin sensitivity.

METABOLIC SYNDROME: A Cluster of Glucose-related Health Challenges

Metabolic syndrome refers to a cluster of diseases, including abdominal obesity, high blood pressure, excessive blood sugar, and abnormal cholesterol levels. We shall study the underlying mechanisms of metabolic syndrome and its association with glucose abnormalities. Lifestyle therapies, including diet adjustments, regular exercise, stress management, and smoking cessation, will be highlighted as successful techniques for managing metabolic syndrome.

OTHER GLUCOSE-RELATED HEALTH CHALLENGES

In addition to diabetes, insulin resistance, and metabolic syndrome, there are other health concerns connected with glucose imbalances. This section will provide an overview of illnesses such as prediabetes, polycystic ovary syndrome

(PCOS), cardiovascular disease, and non-alcoholic fatty liver disease (NAFLD). Practical guidelines for prevention, management, and promoting overall glucose health will be presented for each condition.

STRATEGIES FOR GLUCOSE HEALTH OPTIMIZATION

To optimize glucose health and prevent or manage glucose-related health issues, a holistic strategy is important. This section will highlight essential lifestyle changes, including adopting a balanced and nutritious diet, engaging in regular physical activity, controlling stress levels, obtaining appropriate sleep, and avoiding smoking and excessive alcohol consumption. By applying these techniques, readers can maintain their glucose health and lower the risk of linked health concerns.

Chapter 4

Assessing Your Glucose Health

In this chapter, we will cover numerous ways and tests to check glucose levels and estimate your current health state. By covering this issue fully, we want to address a wide range of health challenges associated with glucose and provide practical solutions and information for optimizing glucose health.

IMPORTANCE OF ASSESSING GLUCOSE HEALTH

Assessing your glucose health is vital for knowing your present state and recognizing any possible glucose-related health concerns. Regular examinations can help detect early indicators of imbalances, check therapy success, and make educated decisions regarding lifestyle improvements. This section will emphasize the necessity of measuring glucose health as a proactive approach to overall well-being.

SELF-MONITORING OF BLOOD GLUCOSE

Self-monitoring of blood glucose (SMBG) is a regularly used method for measuring glucose levels at home. This section will explain the procedure of SMBG, including the use of a blood glucose meter to test blood sugar levels. Practical information on how and when to monitor blood glucose, as well as interpreting the data, will be offered.

CONTINUOUS GLUCOSE MONITORING (CGM)

Continuous glucose monitoring (CGM) is a sophisticated technique that delivers real-time data on glucose levels throughout the day. This section will introduce CGM systems, which use a sensor placed under the skin to assess glucose levels. It will highlight the benefits of CGM, including enhanced glucose control and the ability to track glucose patterns and trends over time.

ORAL GLUCOSE TOLERANCE TEST (OGTT)

The oral glucose tolerance test (OGTT) is a diagnostic test used to determine how your body responds to a concentrated glucose solution. This section will outline the technique, including fasting before the test and ingesting a glucose drink. The interpretation of data, including normal ranges and signs of impaired glucose tolerance or diabetes, will be discussed.

HEMOGLOBIN A1c (HbA1c) TEST

The hemoglobin A1c (HbA1c) test is a routinely used blood test that examines average blood sugar levels over the past two to three months. This section will provide an overview of the HbA1c test, including its importance in diagnosing and monitoring diabetes. It will explain the goal ranges and how to interpret HbA1c values.

OTHER ASSESSMENTS AND TESTS

In addition to the aforementioned measures, there are various examinations and tests that can provide valuable insights into glucose health. This section will discuss alternate metrics such as fructosamine levels, postprandial glucose testing, and fasting plasma glucose assays. It will explore the specific use cases and significance of these tests in assessing glucose health.

INTERPRETING RESULTS AND SEEKING PROFESSIONAL GUIDANCE

Interpreting glucose assessment findings might be challenging. This section will provide information on recognizing the relevance of different glucose metrics, such as blood glucose levels, HbA1c values, and CGM data. It will emphasize the necessity of receiving expert help from healthcare providers, such as endocrinologists or certified diabetes educators, to interpret data appropriately and build tailored treatment programs.

TRACKING AND MONITORING PROGRESS

Tracking and monitoring glucose levels over time can provide significant information into your glucose health. This section will examine ways for tracking and interpreting data from self-monitoring or CGM systems, as well as the benefits of keeping a glucose diary or using digital health apps. It will inspire readers to use these tools to discover patterns, make informed decisions, and measure progress towards glycemic health objectives.

Chapter 5

The Glucose Goddess Diet Principles

In this chapter, we will introduce the key principles and foundations of the Glucose Goddess Diet. The Glucose Goddess Diet focuses on balanced diet and blood sugar management, addressing a wide range of health concerns associated with glucose imbalances. By giving practical solutions and assistance, we want to empower readers to make informed food decisions and enhance their glucose health.

UNDERSTANDING BALANCED NUTRITION

Balanced nutrition constitutes the basis of the Glucose Goddess Diet. This section will emphasize the need of ingesting a range of nutrient-dense foods to suit your body's nutritional needs. It will explain the macronutrients (carbohydrates, proteins, and fats) and micronutrients (vitamins and minerals) necessary for optimal health. Practical ideas for portion control and mindful eating will also be offered.

FOCUS ON COMPLEX CARBOHYDRATES

Complex carbs, such as whole grains, legumes, fruits, and vegetables, play a significant role in the Glucose Goddess Diet. This section will emphasize the benefits of complex carbs, which deliver a slow and constant release of glucose into the bloodstream. It will offer suggestions on adding these foods into meals and snacks, stressing their fiber content and overall nutritional worth.

PROTEIN FOR SATIETY AND BLOOD SUGAR CONTROL

Protein is a vital component of the Glucose Goddess Diet. This section will explain the importance of protein in increasing satiety, supporting muscular health, and balancing blood sugar levels. It will provide recommendations on incorporating lean sources of protein, such as poultry, fish, tofu, and lentils, into meals. Practical recommendations regarding portion sizes and balancing protein consumption will be presented.

EMPHASIZING HEALTHY FATS

Healthy fats are a vital aspect of the Glucose Goddess Diet. This section will discuss the benefits of sources including avocados, almonds, seeds, and olive oil, which supply vital fatty acids and enhance satiety. It will highlight the necessity of moderation and portion control when consuming fats. Practical recommendations for introducing healthy fats into meals will be offered.

THE ROLE OF FIBER IN BLOOD SUGAR MANAGEMENT

Fiber plays a significant function in blood sugar regulation and overall health. This section will highlight the importance of ingesting fiber-rich foods, such as whole grains, vegetables, fruits, and legumes. It will explain how dietary fiber slows down digestion, leading to a more gradual release of glucose into the system. Practical suggestions for boosting fiber intake and selecting high-fiber food choices will be given.

MEAL PLANNING AND BALANCED PLATE METHOD

Meal planning is a crucial tool for executing the Glucose Goddess Diet. This section will provide practical information on producing well-balanced meals using the Balanced Plate Method. It will examine portion sizes and the distribution of macronutrients on a plate, stressing the presence of complex carbohydrates, lean proteins, healthy fats, and veggies. Sample meal planning and food ideas will be provided.

MINDFUL EATING AND LISTENING TO YOUR BODY

Mindful eating is a key component of the Glucose Goddess Diet. This part will emphasize the significance of paying attention to hunger and fullness cues, eating carefully, and relishing food. It will include practical techniques for building mindful eating habits, such as minimizing distractions during meals and practicing gratitude for healthful food choices.

HYDRATION AND BLOOD SUGAR CONTROL

Proper hydration is vital for glucose wellness. This section will highlight the necessity of drinking appropriate water throughout the day and limiting sugary beverages. It will present practical ways for staying hydrated and highlight the benefits of water for general well-being.

Chapter 6

Building a Glucose-Friendly Pantry

IMPORTANCE OF A GLUCOSE-FRIENDLY PANTRY

A glucose-friendly pantry is a cornerstone for keeping a nutritious diet that supports glucose wellness. By stocking your pantry with nutritious items that match with the concepts of the Glucose Goddess Diet, you can make informed and wholesome meal choices. Having a well-stocked pantry decreases dependency on processed foods and ensures you have the required components to produce balanced and healthful meals.

WHOLE GRAINS AND COMPLEX CARBOHYDRATES

Whole grains should be a big element in your glucose-friendly pantry. Opt for alternatives such as whole wheat, brown rice, quinoa, and oats. These whole grains include a plethora of fiber, vitamins, and minerals that are beneficial for glucose health. By including complex carbs into your meals, you can encourage consistent blood sugar levels and enhance overall glucose management. Experiment with recipes that use whole grains, and try using whole grain flours for baking.

PROTEIN SOURCES

A well-rounded glucose-friendly pantry offers a variety of protein sources. Lean meats like chicken, turkey, and fish are wonderful choices. For vegetarian or plant-based options, consider legumes such as lentils, chickpeas, and black beans. Additionally, tofu, tempeh, and eggs can be significant sources of protein. By introducing a diversity of protein sources into your pantry, you can enjoy various and healthy meals while improving satiety and blood sugar control.

HEALTHY FATS AND OILS

Healthy fats play a significant role in a glucose-friendly pantry. Include sources such as avocados, nuts (including almonds, walnuts, and cashews), seeds (such as flaxseeds and chia seeds), olive oil, and coconut oil. These healthy fats supply vital fatty acids and contribute to a satisfying and well-rounded diet. However, moderation is crucial, as fats are abundant in calories. Be aware of portion amounts while using fats and oils in your cooking and meal preparation.

FRESH FRUITS AND VEGETABLES

A glucose-friendly pantry should always have a range of fresh fruits and vegetables. These vivid and nutrient-dense alternatives contain fiber, vitamins, minerals, and antioxidants. Select a choice of colored fruits and vegetables to guarantee you benefit from a varied assortment of nutrients. Consider buying seasonal food and learn suitable storing procedures to keep its freshness for extended periods. Incorporating fruits and vegetables into meals, snacks, and smoothies will assist maintain your glucose wellness.

HERBS, SPICES, AND FLAVOR ENHANCERS

Enhancing the flavors of your foods without relying on excessive salt, sugar, or unhealthy condiments is vital for a glucose-friendly pantry. Herbs and spices, such as basil, oregano, turmeric, cinnamon, and ginger, can add depth and taste to your foods while giving additional health benefits. Experiment with different mixes to produce delectable dinners. Consider incorporating natural flavor enhancers like garlic, onions, citrus fruits, and vinegar to add complexity to your meals.

INGREDIENTS TO AVOID

Maintaining a glucose-friendly pantry entails being cautious of products that can negatively impact glucose health. Refined sugars, high-fructose corn syrup, artificial sweeteners, trans fats, and excessive sodium are among the substances to minimize or avoid. Reading food labels and understanding multiple terms for added sugars can help you make informed decisions. Reduce the consumption of processed foods that are generally heavy in these nutrients and focus on full, unprocessed options.

PANTRY ORGANIZATION AND MEAL PLANNING

Organizing your cupboard in a way that improves glucose health can simplify meal preparation and support your dietary objectives. Keep fundamental foods like nutritious grains, canned beans, and healthy oils easily available. Consider using clear storage containers for bulk materials and marking them for easy identification. Meal planning is a helpful technique for maintaining a glucose-friendly pantry. Plan your meals ahead, make a grocery list, and batch cook when possible to ensure you have healthful meals easily available.

Chapter 7

Meal Planning for Glucose Health

INTRODUCTION TO MEAL PLANNING FOR GLUCOSE HEALTH

Meal planning is a great technique for optimizing glycemic health. By planning balanced, nutritious meal plans, you can stabilize blood sugar levels, reduce cravings, and enhance general well-being. In this chapter, we will provide detailed information on how to build meal plans that enhance glucose health, address a wide range of health concerns, and enable readers to make informed dietary choices.

UNDERSTANDING MACRONUTRIENTS AND BALANCED MEALS

An important component of meal planning for glycemic health is knowing macronutrients and producing balanced meals. This section will describe the importance of carbs, proteins, and lipids in maintaining stable blood sugar levels. It will provide advice on portion sizes and the appropriate distribution of macronutrients in meals to enhance glycemic control and satiety.

INCORPORATING COMPLEX CARBOHYDRATES

Complex carbs are important for stable blood sugar levels. This section will focus on incorporating sources of complex carbs, such as whole grains, legumes, and starchy vegetables, into meal plans. It will include examples of balanced meals that feature these nutrient-rich foods, along with portion suggestions.

BALANCING PROTEIN INTAKE

Protein serves a critical role in increasing satiety and maintaining blood sugar levels. This section will explore diverse protein sources, including lean meats, poultry, fish, eggs, legumes, and plant-based choices. It will provide recommendations on the optimal portion sizes and how to add protein into each meal to maintain a well-balanced diet.

INCLUDING HEALTHY FATS

Healthy fats are an important component of meal planning for glycemic health. This section will emphasize sources of healthy fats, such as avocados, nuts, seeds, and olive oil, and their benefits for blood sugar regulation. It will include tips on incorporating healthy fats into meals and snacks, along with portion recommendations.

PRIORITIZING FIBER-RICH FOODS

Fiber-rich foods are vital for sustaining stable blood sugar levels and overall health. This section will emphasize the necessity of including fruits, vegetables, whole grains, and legumes in meal plans to enhance fiber consumption. It will provide practical advice on how to incorporate these items into meals and snacks for optimal glucose health.

GLYCEMIC INDEX AND GLYCEMIC LOAD

Understanding the glycemic index (GI) and glycemic load (GL) of foods might aid with meal planning for glucose wellness. This section will explain the principles of GI and GL and how they affect blood sugar levels. It will provide advice on choosing low-GI and low-GL foods to help stable blood sugar control.

MEAL PREPPING AND BATCH COOKING

Meal preparing and bulk cooking are useful practices for efficient meal planning. This section will examine the benefits of preparing meals in advance and provide practical advice for efficient meal prepping. It will offer tips on how to plan and cook meals in batches to save time and guarantee that healthy selections are easily available.

SNACK IDEAS FOR GLUCOSE HEALTH

Including healthy snacks in your meal plan will help minimize blood sugar falls and lessen cravings. This section will present a variety of snack choices that are balanced and supportive of glycemic health. It will emphasize the significance of choosing nutrient-dense snacks and offer suggestions for quick and easy options.

MINDFUL EATING AND PORTION CONTROL

Mindful eating and portion control are crucial to meal planning for glycemic health. This section will stress the significance of being present at meals, listening to hunger and fullness cues, and exercising portion management. It will offer practical advice and tactics for building mindful eating habits and maintaining optimal portion sizes.

FLEXIBILITY AND INDIVIDUALIZATION

Meal planning should be flexible and suited to individual needs and interests. This section will emphasize the significance of listening to your body, experimenting with different foods, and altering meal plans accordingly. It will encourage users to work with healthcare providers or registered dietitians to establish individualized meal plans based on unique health concerns and nutritional requirements.

Chapter 8

Glucose Goddess Diet Recipes

In this chapter, we present a range of delicious and easy-to-prepare meals that match with the concepts of the Glucose Goddess Diet. These recipes focus on balanced nutrition, blood sugar management, and promoting general health. By giving practical answers and assistance, we seek to address a wide range of health concerns associated with glucose imbalances and empower readers to enjoy delectable meals while supporting their glucose health.

BREAKFAST RECIPES

Breakfast is a vital meal for starting the day on the right foot. These breakfast recipes are designed to deliver continuous energy, satiety, and stable blood sugar levels.

RECIPE 1: Veggie Omelet with Spinach and Mushrooms

This protein-packed omelet is loaded with nutrient-rich vegetables and herbs, delivering a delightful and gratifying start to your day.

RECIPE 2: Overnight Chia Pudding with Berries

This make-ahead dish mixes chia seeds, almond milk, and berries to produce a creamy and fiber-rich breakfast alternative. It's a terrific way to add omega-3 fatty acids and antioxidants into your morning routine.

LUNCH RECIPES

Lunchtime asks for wholesome and balanced meals that keep you energized throughout the day. These lunch recipes provide a variety of options to suit varied tastes and dietary preferences.

RECIPE 1: Quinoa Salad with Roasted Vegetables and Lemon-Tahini Dressing

This bright salad mixes protein-rich quinoa, roasted veggies, and a tart lemon-tahini sauce. It's a pleasant and nutritious alternative for a lunchtime meal.

RECIPE 2: Lentil Soup with Vegetables

This hearty lentil soup is packed with fiber, protein, and an array of vegetables. It's a comfortable and nourishing option that supports stable blood sugar levels.

DINNER RECIPES

Dinner is an opportunity to eat delectable foods while nourishing your body with healthful nutrients. These meal recipes feature a variety of flavors and textures to please your taste senses.

RECIPE 1: Baked Salmon with Lemon and Dill

This simple yet gorgeous meal comprises baked salmon filets seasoned with fresh lemon juice and dill. It's a great source of omega-3 fatty acids and high-quality protein.

RECIPE 2: Roasted Chicken Breast with Herbs and Vegetables

This roasted chicken breast is complimented by a medley of seasonal vegetables, producing a healthful and fulfilling supper alternative. The herbs offer depth of taste and enrich the whole meal experience.

SNACK RECIPES

Healthy snacks can help minimize blood sugar falls and control cravings between meals. These snack dishes offer a blend of nutrients and flavors to keep you satiated throughout the day.

RECIPE 1: Greek Yogurt Parfait with Berries and Almonds

This delightful and protein-packed parfait mixes Greek yogurt, juicy berries, and crispy almonds. It's a quick and easy snack that includes a combination of fiber, antioxidants, and healthy fats.

RECIPE 2: Roasted Chickpeas with Spices

Roasted chickpeas seasoned with an array of spices make for a crispy and protein-rich snack. They are an excellent alternative to processed treats and give a pleasing texture.

DESSERT RECIPES

Enjoying a sweet treat doesn't have to compromise your glucose wellness. These dessert recipes offer healthier choices that yet fulfill your needs.

RECIPE 1: Dark Chocolate Avocado Mousse

This creamy and decadent mousse is created with ripe avocados and dark chocolate, giving a rich source of healthy fats and antioxidants. It's a guilt-free dessert alternative that won't increase your blood sugar levels.

RECIPE 2: Baked Apples with Cinnamon and Walnuts

This warm and comforting dish has baked apples topped with a dusting of cinnamon and crushed walnuts. It's a simple yet delightful alternative that highlights the natural sweetness of apples.

RECIPE ADAPTATIONS AND MODIFICATIONS

We appreciate that dietary choices and limits may vary among individuals. In this part, we present suggestions and changes for the recipes to fit diverse dietary demands. Whether you practice a vegetarian, vegan, gluten-free, or dairy-free diet, there are solutions to meet your preferences and ensure you can still enjoy the great flavors while maintaining your glucose health.

BONUS CHAPTER

BREAKFAST RECIPES:

1. Veggie Omelet with Spinach and Mushrooms:

INGREDIENTS:

2 eggs

Handful of spinach leaves

Sliced mushrooms

Chopped onion

Chopped bell peppers

Salt and pepper to taste

Olive oil for cooking

Instructions:

1. In a bowl, whisk the eggs until fully beaten. Season with salt and pepper.

2. Heat olive oil in a non-stick pan over medium heat.

3. Add onions, bell peppers, and mushrooms to the pan. Sauté until vegetables are tender.

4. Add spinach leaves and simmer until wilted.

5. Pour the beaten eggs over the veggies in the pan. Cook until the omelet is set and lightly browned on the bottom.

6. Flip the omelet or fold it in half. Cook for another minute or until the eggs are cooked through.

7. Serve hot and enjoy!

2. Overnight Chia Pudding with Berries:

INGREDIENTS:

2 teaspoons chia seeds

1/2 cup almond milk (or other non-dairy milk of your choice)

1 teaspoon honey or maple syrup (optional)

Fresh berries for topping

INSTRUCTIONS:

1. In a jar or bowl, blend chia seeds and almond milk. Stir carefully to ensure the chia seeds are uniformly dispersed.

2. If preferred, add honey or maple syrup for sweetness. Stir again.

3. Cover the jar or bowl and refrigerate overnight or for at least 4 hours.

4. When ready to serve, give the chia pudding a good stir. If it appears too thick, you can add a bit more almond milk.

5. Top with fresh berries and enjoy!

LUNCH RECIPES:

1. Quinoa Salad with Roasted Vegetables and Lemon-Tahini Dressing:

INGREDIENTS:

1 cup cooked quinoa

Assorted roasted veggies (e.g., bell peppers, zucchini, eggplant, cherry tomatoes)

Handful of fresh herbs (such as parsley or basil)

Lemon-Tahini Dressing:

2 tablespoons tahini Juice of 1 lemon

1 tablespoon olive oil

1 garlic clove, minced

Salt and pepper to taste

INSTRUCTIONS:

1. Preheat the oven to 400°F (200°C).

2. Toss the vegetables with olive oil, salt, and pepper, then lay them on a baking sheet. Roast in the preheated oven for about 20 minutes or until tender and slightly browned.

3. In a large bowl, combine the cooked quinoa, roasted veggies, and fresh herbs.

4. In a separate small bowl, whisk together the tahini, lemon juice, olive oil, minced garlic, salt, and pepper to make the dressing.

5. Pour the Lemon-Tahini Dressing over the quinoa and vegetables. Toss well to coat.

6. Serve the quinoa salad at room temperature or chilled.

2. Lentil Soup with Vegetables:

INGREDIENTS:

1 cup dry lentils

Assorted veggies (e.g., carrots, celery, onions, kale)

4 cups vegetable broth

2 cloves garlic, minced

1 teaspoon cumin

1 teaspoon turmeric

Salt and pepper to taste

Fresh lemon juice (optional, for serving)

INSTRUCTIONS:

1. Rinse the lentils and remove any debris. Set aside.

2. In a large pot, sauté the minced garlic in olive oil until aromatic.

3. Add the vegetables to the saucepan and boil for a few minutes until they start to soften.

4. Add the lentils, vegetable broth, cumin, turmeric, salt, and pepper to the pot. Stir well to mix.

5. Bring the soup to a boil, then reduce the heat and allow it simmer for about 30-40 minutes or until the lentils are cooked.

6. Adjust the seasoning as needed.

7. Serve the lentil soup hot, and squeeze fresh lemon juice over each bowl if preferred.

SNACK RECIPES:

1. Greek Yogurt Parfait with Berries and Almonds:

INGREDIENTS:

1 cup Greek yogurtAssorted fresh berries (such as strawberries, blueberries, raspberries)

Handful of almonds, chopped

Drizzle of honey (optional)

INSTRUCTIONS:

1. In a glass or bowl, layer Greek yogurt, fresh berries, and sliced almonds.

2. Repeat the layers until all ingredients are utilized.

3. If preferred, sprinkle a little honey over the top for extra sweetness.

4. Serve the Greek Yogurt Parfait immediately and enjoy!

3. Roasted Chickpeas with Spices:

INGREDIENTS:

1 can chickpeas, drained and rinsed

1 tablespoon olive oil

1 teaspoon paprika

1/2 teaspoon cumin

1/2 teaspoon garlic powder

1/4 teaspoon cayenne pepper (optional, for heat)

Salt and pepper to taste

INSTRUCTIONS:

1. Preheat the oven to 400°F (200°C).

2. Pat the chickpeas dry with a paper towel to eliminate extra moisture.

3. In a bowl, combine the chickpeas with olive oil, paprika, cumin, garlic powder, cayenne pepper (if using), salt, and pepper.

4. Spread the seasoned chickpeas on a baking sheet in a single layer.

5. Roast in the preheated oven for about 25-30 minutes, shaking the pan occasionally, until the chickpeas are crispy and golden.

6. Remove from the oven and let them cool slightly before serving.

7. Enjoy the roasted chickpeas as a crispy and protein-rich snack.

Remember to alter these recipes based on your specific preferences and nutritional restrictions. Experiment with different flavors and ingredients to produce a range of meals that match with the Glucose Control Diet Method guidelines.

Chapter 9

Managing Cravings and Emotional Eating

In this chapter, we go into the topic of regulating cravings and emotional eating. We examine techniques to overcome these barriers and establish healthy dietary habits, empowering readers to make conscious choices. By addressing a wide range of health concerns associated with cravings and emotional eating, we provide practical answers and counseling to enhance overall well-being. The material supplied is factual, evidence-based, and geared towards ensuring credibility.

UNDERSTANDING CRAVINGS

To properly manage cravings, it is vital to understand their underlying origins. This section discusses the different elements that lead to cravings, including physiological, psychological, and environmental causes. By obtaining understanding into the core reasons of cravings, readers can begin to build techniques for managing and diminishing them.

IDENTIFYING EMOTIONAL EATING PATTERNS

Emotional eating is a frequent response to stress, boredom, melancholy, or other emotions. This section focuses on helping readers identify emotional eating patterns and recognize the connection between their emotions and food choices. By growing self-awareness, readers can break free from the cycle of emotional eating and make more mindful decisions regarding their food consumption.

STRATEGIES TO MANAGE CRAVINGS

This section contains practical ways to help readers better handle urges. These strategies include:

1. Mindful Eating: Practicing mindfulness during meals can enhance the eating experience and help individuals detect actual hunger vs urges. By paying attention to bodily hunger indicators and relishing each bite, readers can create a healthier relationship with food.

2. Balanced Meals: Ensuring that meals are balanced with a variety of protein, healthy fats, and complex carbohydrates can help stabilize blood sugar levels and prevent cravings. This section includes tips on constructing balanced meals that encourage satiety and promote stable energy levels.

3. Hydration: Staying adequately hydrated is key for regulating cravings. Sometimes, the body misinterprets thirst as hunger, leading to unnecessary munching. Encouraging readers to drink appropriate water throughout the day can help reduce dehydration-related cravings.

4. Planning Ahead: Planning meals and snacks in advance helps lessen the risk of impulsive and

unhealthy eating choices. This section gives advice on meal preparing, creating grocery lists, and having nutritious snacks easily available to enhance mindful eating.

Section 9.5: Coping with Emotional Eating

Managing emotional eating needs other coping mechanisms for dealing with emotions. This section contains practical suggestions to help readers develop healthier ways of treating their emotions, including:

1. Emotional Awareness: Encouraging readers to identify and express their feelings without relying on food can be revolutionary. This section discusses approaches such as writing, meditation,

or seeking support from loved ones or therapists to develop emotional awareness.

2. Finding Alternatives: Suggesting alternative activities to replace emotional eating will help refocus attention away from food. Engaging in hobbies, physical exercise, deep breathing techniques, or other stress-reducing activities can give healthy avenues for emotional expression.

3. Building a Support System: Having a support system can make a major difference in managing emotional eating. This section emphasizes the value of surrounding oneself with understanding and helpful individuals who may offer encouragement and assistance during hard times.

4. receiving Professional support: For individuals struggling with severe emotional eating or disordered eating patterns, receiving professional support from a therapist or registered dietitian specializing in emotional eating might be beneficial. These professionals can provide specialized techniques and help to treat underlying emotional disorders.

CULTIVATING A POSITIVE RELATIONSHIP WITH FOOD

Developing a positive relationship with food is crucial for long-term success in regulating cravings and emotional eating. This section focuses on promoting a healthy mentality and encouraging readers to:

1. Practice Self-Compassion: Encouraging self-compassion is vital in overcoming guilt or shame connected with cravings and emotional eating. Readers are reminded that everyone has periodic mistakes, and treating themselves with care and empathy is vital for progress.

2. Practice Intuitive Eating: Intuitive eating involves listening to one's body cues, acknowledging hunger and fullness, and permitting all foods in moderation. This section includes information on reconnecting with internal cues and trusting the body's wisdom in making food decisions.

3. Focus on nourishing: Shifting the mentality from limitation to nourishing can transform the

relationship with food. Encouraging readers to focus on sustaining their bodies with nutrient-dense foods while allowing occasional pleasures can foster a healthy and balanced approach to eating.

4. Celebrate Non-Food Rewards: Encouraging readers to celebrate triumphs or reward themselves without turning to food might help remove the relationship between emotions and eating. This section provides alternate non-food rewards, such as treating oneself to a massage, engaging in a hobby, or spending quality time with loved ones.

Chapter 10

Exercise and Glucose Health

In this chapter, we investigate the crucial function of physical activity in glucose regulation. Regular exercise gives several benefits for overall health and plays a vital role in maintaining stable blood sugar levels. By addressing a wide range of health concerns associated with glucose health, we provide practical answers and information to encourage readers to incorporate exercise into their lifestyle. The material offered is factual, evidence-based, and focused on guaranteeing credibility.

UNDERSTANDING THE BENEFITS OF EXERCISE FOR GLUCOSE HEALTH

Regular exercise has a tremendous impact on glucose management and general health. This section discusses the benefits of exercise, such as:

1. Improved Insulin Sensitivity: Exercise raises the body's sensitivity to insulin, allowing for greater use of glucose and improved blood sugar control.

2. Weight Management: Physical activity helps manage weight, reducing the chance of developing insulin resistance and type 2 diabetes.

3. Cardiovascular Health: Exercise strengthens the heart and cardiovascular system, reducing

the risk of cardiovascular disorders usually connected with glucose imbalances.

4. Stress Reduction: Regular exercise can help reduce stress levels, which can lead to better glucose regulation.

TYPES OF EXERCISE FOR GLUCOSE HEALTH

Different sorts of exercise can contribute to glycemic wellness. This section discusses numerous workout modalities and their benefits:

1. Aerobic Exercise: Activities including brisk walking, jogging, swimming, cycling, and dancing boost heart rate and enhance cardiovascular fitness. Aerobic exercise helps burn calories, regulate weight, and increase insulin sensitivity.

2. Strength Training: Resistance activities, such as weightlifting or utilizing resistance bands, enhance muscle growth and strength. Building muscular mass promotes insulin sensitivity and glucose consumption.

3. High-Intensity Interval Training (HIIT): HIIT involves short bursts of intensive activity alternated with intervals of rest or low-intensity exercise. HIIT workouts are time-efficient and have been demonstrated to improve glycemic control and cardiovascular fitness.

4. Flexibility and Balance Exercises: Stretching exercises, yoga, and balance training increase flexibility, range of motion, and stability. These

exercises can be good for overall well-being and injury prevention.

EXERCISE RECOMMENDATIONS FOR BEGINNERS

For individuals new to exercise or those with unique health concerns, it's crucial to start gradually and choose exercises that are acceptable for their fitness level. This section contains exercise advice for beginners:

1. Consultation with Healthcare specialists: Before starting an exercise program, persons with underlying health concerns should meet with their healthcare specialists for personalized counsel and recommendations.

2. Start Slowly: Beginners should start with low-impact exercises such as walking or swimming. Gradually increase the duration and intensity of the workouts over time.

3. Consistency is Key: Aim for at least 150 minutes of moderate-intensity aerobic exercise or 75 minutes of vigorous-intensity aerobic exercise every week. Spread the workout sessions throughout the week for best advantages.

4. Strength Training: Include strength training activities at least two days a week, emphasizing key muscle groups. Use light weights or resistance bands and focus on appropriate form and technique.

5. Listen to Your Body: Pay attention to how your body responds to exercise. If you suffer any pain or discomfort, adapt the activity or check with a fitness specialist.

SAFETY CONSIDERATIONS AND PRECAUTIONS

Exercise is typically safe for most individuals, although certain care should be followed. This section provides safety considerations:

1. Warm-up and Cool-down: Always begin each exercise session with a warm-up to prepare the body for physical activity and end with a cool-down to allow for progressive recovery.

2. Hydration: Drink water before, during, and after exercise to stay hydrated.

3. Proper Gear: Wear suitable footwear and gear that provides support and comfort throughout exercising.

4. Blood Sugar Monitoring: Individuals with diabetes or glucose imbalances should check their blood sugar levels before, during, and after exercise. Adjustments to medication or dietary consumption may be necessary.

5. Seek Professional help: If unsure about proper exercise form, technique, or individual needs, consider seeking help from a trained fitness professional or personal trainer.

MAKING EXERCISE ENJOYABLE AND SUSTAINABLE

To achieve long-term adherence to a workout regimen, it's crucial to select activities that are pleasurable and sustainable. This section provides ways to make exercise a positive experience:

1. Find Activities You Enjoy: Choose exercises that you actually enjoy and look forward to. This might be dancing, hiking, riding, or any activity that offers you delight.

2. Buddy System: Exercise with a friend or attend a group fitness class to bring social connection and accountability to your routine.

3. Set Realistic Goals: Set reasonable goals that correspond with your talents and progressively

grow from there. Celebrate milestones and acknowledge your progress.

4. Variety and Fun: Incorporate different sorts of exercises to keep your program interesting and prevent monotony. Explore new things and try different classes or fitness videos.

5. Listen to Music or Podcasts: Create a playlist or listen to podcasts throughout your workouts to make them more fun and distract from any discomfort.

Chapter 11

Lifestyle Factors and Glucose Health

Maintaining balanced glucose levels is vital for overall health and well-being. While nutrition and exercise are generally known elements impacting glucose regulation, various lifestyle factors, including sleep, stress, and others, can dramatically affect your blood sugar levels. In this detailed book, we will investigate the intricate relationship between lifestyle factors and glucose health. We will address the impact of sleep deprivation, chronic stress, sedentary activity, and other lifestyle choices on glucose regulation.

Additionally, we will share practical tips and evidence-based guidelines for maintaining a balanced lifestyle that supports optimal glucose control.

THE IMPACT OF SLEEP ON GLUCOSE REGULATION:

Adequate sleep serves a critical role in maintaining healthy glucose levels. Sleep deprivation has been associated with poor glucose metabolism, insulin resistance, and an increased risk of developing type 2 diabetes. When we lack sufficient sleep, our body's capacity to manage glucose gets weakened. This can lead to higher blood sugar levels and a greater chance of getting diabetes over time.

To Promote Healthy Glucose Regulation Through Sleep, Here Are Some Tips:

1. Aim for 7-9 hours of decent sleep each night.

2. Establish a consistent sleep habit by going to bed and waking up at the same time every day.

3. Create a sleep-friendly environment by ensuring your bedroom is dark, quiet, and at a suitable temperature.

4. Limit exposure to electronic devices, such as smartphones and tablets, before bedtime, as the blue light emitted can disrupt sleep patterns.

5. Avoid taking caffeine or engaging in stimulating activities close to bedtime.

The Impact Of Stress On Glucose Regulation: Chronic stress can greatly impair glucose regulation and raise the risk of acquiring diabetes. When we encounter stress, our body releases stress chemicals, such as cortisol and adrenaline, which can boost blood sugar levels. Prolonged exposure to high amounts of stress hormones can lead to insulin resistance and difficulty in maintaining stable glucose levels.

To Manage Stress Effectively And Support Glucose Health, Consider The Following Strategies:

1. Practice stress-reducing strategies, such as deep breathing exercises, meditation, or yoga.

2. Engage in regular physical activity, as exercise can help reduce stress and improve better glucose management.

3. Prioritize self-care activities that bring you joy and relaxation, such as spending time with loved

ones, pursuing hobbies, or engaging in creative outlets.

4. Seek support from friends, family, or professional counselors to help manage and cope with stress.

5. Establish healthy boundaries and learn to say no to excessive commitments or duties that may add to stress.

OTHER LIFESTYLE FACTORS AND GLUCOSE HEALTH:

Apart from sleep and stress, several other lifestyle factors can affect glucose regulation:

1. Physical Activity: Regular exercise improves insulin sensitivity, aids in weight management, and promotes healthy glucose levels. Aim for at

least 150 minutes of moderate-intensity aerobic activity per week, along with strength training activities.

2. Diet: A balanced diet rich in whole grains, fruits, vegetables, lean proteins, and healthy fats can support glucose management. Limit the consumption of sugary foods, refined carbs, and processed snacks. Consider speaking with a trained nutritionist for personalized nutritional suggestions.

3. Sedentary Behavior: Prolonged durations of sitting or sedentary behavior can negatively affect glucose regulation. Incorporate regular movement throughout the day, such as taking

brief walks, stretching breaks, or standing while working.

4. Weight Management: Maintaining a healthy weight is vital for glucose wellness. If overweight, even modest weight loss can increase insulin sensitivity and lessen the chance of developing diabetes.

5. Smoking and Alcohol use: Smoking and excessive alcohol use can both impair glucose control. Quitting smoking and reducing alcohol intake are excellent for overall health and glucose control.

Chapter 12

Monitoring and Tracking Progress

Monitoring and tracking glucose levels are vital for persons aiming to maintain optimal glucose control and manage their overall health. Regular monitoring allows individuals to obtain useful insights into their glucose swings, make informed decisions, and take essential changes to ensure long-term success. In this detailed tutorial, we will cover the necessity of monitoring glucose levels, measuring progress, and creating reasonable objectives. By covering a wide range of health concerns relating to this topic and giving evidence-based solutions, we want to empower readers with practical assistance for efficiently regulating their glucose levels.

THE IMPORTANCE OF MONITORING GLUCOSE LEVELS:

Monitoring glucose levels helps individuals obtain a comprehensive picture of their present blood sugar state and how their body responds to diverse stimuli, including as meals, physical exercise, and medications. By monitoring periodically, individuals can:

1. Identify Patterns: Regular monitoring permits the identification of patterns in glucose levels, such as the impact of various diets, exercise routines, or stresses. This information helps

individuals to make informed choices and adapt their lifestyle accordingly.

2. Detecting Abnormalities: Monitoring allows individuals to notice high or low blood sugar levels swiftly. Identifying these irregularities can assist avert consequences and allow an opportunity to take appropriate corrective actions, such as injecting insulin or consuming glucose-raising meals.

3. Assess Treatment Efficacy: For persons managing diabetes, monitoring glucose levels provides information into the effectiveness of their treatment strategy, including medications, insulin therapy, or dietary changes. By tracking their reaction to interventions, individuals can

cooperate with healthcare practitioners to make required adjustments for optimal glucose management.

TIPS FOR EFFECTIVE GLUCOSE MONITORING:

To Ensure Accurate And Reliable Glucose Monitoring, Consider The Following Tips:

1. Choose a Suitable Glucose Monitoring Device: Select a glucose monitoring device that meets your needs, interests, and lifestyle. There are several choices available, including standard glucose meters, continuous glucose monitoring (CGM) systems, and flash glucose monitoring devices. Consult with your healthcare physician to decide the best suited device for your case.

2. Establish a Monitoring regimen: Develop a consistent monitoring regimen that matches with your healthcare provider's recommendations. Regularly measure your glucose levels at certain times throughout the day, such as before and after meals, before exercise, and before night.

3. Record and Track Results: Keep a record of your glucose readings and other pertinent information, such as meals, medications, physical activity, and symptoms. Utilize a diary, mobile app, or digital platform to measure your progress over time. This record will provide a detailed summary of your glucose control and assist discover patterns or areas for improvement.

THE IMPORTANCE OF TRACKING PROGRESS:

Tracking progress is a crucial component of glucose management. It helps individuals to analyze their efforts, find areas of improvement, and celebrate triumphs. By tracking progress, individuals can:

1. Identify Successes and Challenges: Tracking progress helps individuals acknowledge their achievements, such as consistent glucose control, improved living choices, or weight management. It also indicates difficulties, such as periods of uncontrolled glucose levels or specific triggers for variations.

2. Stay Motivated: Regularly assessing progress can act as a source of inspiration. Witnessing gains and good trends underscores the worth of

continuous efforts and motivates individuals to continue their commitment to glucose management.

3. Collaborate with Healthcare Providers: Progress tracking gives essential data for healthcare providers to evaluate the success of the treatment plan and make appropriate adjustments. By sharing progress reports with their healthcare team, individuals can receive individualized direction and support.

TIPS FOR EFFECTIVE PROGRESS TRACKING:
To Track Progress Effectively, Consider Implementing The Following Strategies:
1. Set Specific Goals: Establish quantifiable and achievable goals linked to glucose management,

such as maintaining a target range of blood sugar levels, increasing physical activity, or adopting healthier eating habits. Break down enormous ambitions into smaller, attainable actions.

2. Utilize Technology: Utilize digital tools, mobile apps, or wearable gadgets to streamline progress tracking. These programs often contain functionality for recording glucose levels, physical activity, meals, and other important data. Additionally, they may offer visualization tools and trend analysis for improved understanding and interpretation of progress.

3. Regularly Review and Reflect: Take time to review your progress regularly. Assess your achievements, obstacles, and any patterns

observed. Reflect on what has worked well and areas that want change. Use this information to refine your goals and strategy moving ahead.

SETTING ACHIEVABLE GOALS FOR LONG-TERM SUCCESS:

Setting reasonable goals is key for sustaining long-term success in glucose management. Consider the following guidelines while developing goals:

1. Be Realistic: Set goals that are tough yet doable. Avoid creating unrealistic expectations that may lead to dissatisfaction or discouragement.

2. Prioritize: Identify the most crucial areas for improvement based on your personal circumstances and healthcare provider's suggestions. Focus on addressing those issues first before expanding to other goals.

3. Make SMART Goals: Use the SMART framework for defining goals—specific, measurable, achievable, relevant, and time-bound. This framework gives an organized strategy that increases the likelihood of success.

4. Celebrate Milestones: Acknowledge and celebrate victories along the path, regardless of their magnitude. Recognizing progress promotes motivation and reinforces positive habits.

Chapter 13

Special Considerations:

Glucose management is a vital element of overall health, and it becomes much more important in specific health disorders or situations that demand personalized interventions. Factors such as pregnancy, aging, and certain medical diseases might alter glucose regulation and demand unique tactics for effective treatment. In this thorough guide, we will discuss a wide range of health concerns associated with glucose management in these unique circumstances. By giving practical answers and evidence-based guidance, we want to empower readers with the information necessary to traverse these special issues and achieve optimal glucose management.

GLUCOSE MANAGEMENT DURING PREGNANCY: Pregnancy offers unique issues for glucose management, since hormonal changes and the growing fetus might alter blood sugar levels. Gestational diabetes, a disorder characterized by high blood sugar levels during pregnancy, requires specific treatment. Here are some practical ways for regulating glucose levels during pregnancy:

1. Regular Glucose Monitoring: Pregnant individuals with gestational diabetes should measure their blood sugar levels routinely to ensure they remain within goal ranges. This may

involve evaluating fasting levels, postprandial levels (after meals), or as suggested by healthcare providers.

2. Balanced Diet: A well-balanced diet is vital for maintaining glucose control throughout pregnancy. Focus on ingesting nutrient-dense foods, including whole grains, lean meats, fruits, veggies, and healthy fats. Portion control and distributing meals throughout the day can also help normalize blood sugar levels.

3. Physical Activity: Engaging in regular physical activity, as advised by healthcare specialists, can aid in glucose management throughout pregnancy. Consult with a healthcare expert to

establish suitable exercises that are safe for both the individual and the baby.

4. Medications or Insulin: In some circumstances, lifestyle adjustments alone may not be adequate to regulate glucose levels during pregnancy. Healthcare providers may administer medicines or insulin therapy to maintain optimal blood sugar control.

GLUCOSE MANAGEMENT IN AGING: As individuals age, glucose management becomes increasingly important due to changes in metabolism and probable age-related health issues. Here are some practical options for glucose management in older adults:

1. Regular Health Check-ups: Older persons should undertake regular health check-ups to monitor their glucose levels and identify any potential health issues that may impair glucose management. This may include screening for diabetes or prediabetes.

2. Healthy Diet: A balanced and nutritious diet has a significant role in glucose regulation for older persons. Emphasize entire foods, including fruits, vegetables, whole grains, lean meats, and healthy fats. Limit the intake of processed foods, sugary snacks, and beverages.

3. Physical Activity: Engaging in regular physical activity, as advised by healthcare practitioners, is good for older persons in maintaining glucose

control. Activities such as walking, swimming, or tai chi can be gentle yet effective solutions.

4. Medication Management: Older persons may be taking many drugs, some of which can alter glucose levels. It is crucial to speak with healthcare experts to ensure that drug regimens are coordinated to minimize any harmful effects on glucose management.

GLUCOSE MANAGEMENT IN MEDICAL CONDITIONS:

Certain medical problems demand specialized approaches to glucose management. Here are some instances and real solutions for persons with specific health conditions:

1. Type 1 Diabetes: Individuals with type 1 diabetes require insulin therapy to maintain their glucose levels. Regular glucose testing, carbohydrate counting, and insulin injection are critical components of their management. Continuous glucose monitoring devices (CGMs) can provide real-time glucose readings and assist individuals make informed decisions.

2. Type 2 Diabetes: Lifestyle adjustments are critical for managing type 2 diabetes. This includes adopting a balanced diet, engaging in regular physical activity, monitoring glucose levels, and, in certain situations, taking oral medicines or insulin. Regular check-ups with healthcare experts are critical for assessing

progress and changing treatment programs as needed.

3. Prediabetes: Individuals with prediabetes have higher-than-normal blood sugar levels but not yet at the threshold of diabetes. Lifestyle adjustments, including healthy diet, frequent exercise, and weight management, can help prevent or delay the onset of type 2 diabetes. Regular glucose monitoring and follow-up with healthcare experts are crucial.

4. Other Medical disorders: Certain medical disorders, such as polycystic ovarian syndrome (PCOS), cardiovascular disease, or kidney illness, might alter glucose regulation. It is vital to engage closely with healthcare specialists that

specialize in these illnesses to develop specific strategies for glucose management.

Chapter 14

Seeking Professional Guidance:

Taking control of one's health is an important component of enjoying a satisfying life, especially when facing health issues such as diabetes, endocrine diseases, or the need for dietary alterations. While online sites and self-help materials can give significant insights, the necessity of obtaining expert counsel cannot be emphasized. In this comprehensive book, we will cover the critical role of healthcare professionals, including endocrinologists, dietitians, and diabetes educators, in offering tailored guidance and assistance. By addressing a wide range of health concerns and giving evidence-based solutions, this content seeks to empower readers on their health journey and inspire them to seek expert help when needed.

THE EXPERTISE OF ENDOCRINOLOGISTS:

Endocrinologists are medical experts that specialize in the diagnosis, treatment, and management of endocrine disorders, which span a wide spectrum of problems connected to hormones and metabolism. Consulting with an endocrinologist offers various benefits:

1. Accurate Diagnosis: Endocrine problems can present with complex symptoms, making an accurate diagnosis problematic. Endocrinologists offer in-depth expertise and experience in recognizing and differentiating various disorders,

ensuring accurate diagnosis and appropriate treatment approaches.

2. Specialized Treatment Plans: Endocrinologists design customized treatment plans based on an individual's specific needs, including criteria such as age, overall health, and the severity of the problem. These strategies frequently incorporate a combination of medication, lifestyle adjustments, and regular monitoring to optimize health outcomes.

3. Expert Monitoring and Management: Endocrine problems require long-term management and monitoring. Endocrinologists provide extensive follow-up care, monitoring hormone levels, changing therapy regimens, and

offering advice on managing potential consequences. Their knowledge ensures that clients receive the most appropriate and effective care throughout their health journey.

THE ROLE OF DIETITIANS: Dietitians serve a critical role in delivering evidence-based dietary recommendations, making them useful tools for those looking to improve their health or manage illnesses such as diabetes. Here are significant reasons to meet with a dietitian:

1. Personalized Meal Plans: Dietitians evaluate an individual's specific dietary requirements, medical history, and lifestyle when establishing personalized meal plans. This strategy ensures

that nutritional needs are satisfied while addressing specific health concerns or goals.

2. Diabetes Management: For persons with diabetes, dietitians offer specialized understanding in carbohydrate counting, blood sugar management, and glycemic control. They educate patients on the importance of a balanced diet, individualize meal plans, and support them in making smart food choices to maintain stable blood sugar levels.

3. Weight Management: Achieving and maintaining a healthy weight is vital for general well-being. Dietitians provide evidence-based treatments, behavior modification techniques, and continuing support to help clients accomplish

their weight control objectives while prioritizing their health.

DIABETES EDUCATORS: Diabetes educators are healthcare professionals trained in teaching patients with diabetes to effectively manage their disease. Their experience gives crucial support in numerous aspects of diabetes care:

1. Self-Management Education: Diabetes educators educate individuals with the knowledge and skills needed to manage their illness effectively. They provide teaching on blood glucose monitoring, medication management, insulin administration, and lifestyle adjustments. By understanding their health

better, individuals can make educated decisions and actively engage in their care.

2. Problem-Solving and Coping Strategies: Living with diabetes can present daily problems. Diabetes educators help individuals acquire problem-solving abilities and coping strategies to navigate diverse scenarios, such as regulating blood sugar variations, dealing with stress, and making healthy choices in social contexts.

3. Continuous Support: Diabetes educators offer continuing support, answering questions, resolving problems, and offering incentive to those with diabetes. This assistance extends beyond the initial education phase, ensuring

long-term commitment to self-care behaviors and promoting excellent health outcomes.

THE VALUE OF PROFESSIONAL GUIDANCE:

Seeking expert counsel is crucial for various reasons, regardless of the specific health difficulty that individuals may encounter. Here are the primary advantages:

1. Evidence-Based Approach: Healthcare professionals base their recommendations on the latest research and clinical guidelines. By speaking with professionals, individuals can get accurate and up-to-date information, ensuring that their choices coincide with the most credible facts.

2. Personalized Advice: Every individual is unique, and healthcare professionals acknowledge this. They take into account an individual's medical history, current health state, lifestyle, and personal preferences while providing advice. This personalized method guarantees that recommendations are tailored to an individual's specific needs, optimizing outcomes.

3. Holistic Care: Health difficulties can involve numerous aspects, such as physical, emotional, and social factors. Healthcare experts give comprehensive care by addressing these various areas. They consider the individual as a whole and give complete support to increase overall well-being.

Chapter 15

Maintaining Long-Term Glucose Health:

As your endocrinologist, my goal is to provide you with practical techniques and support to preserve long-term glucose health. Managing glucose levels is critical for persons with diabetes or those at risk of getting the condition. By adopting a healthy lifestyle and applying appropriate diabetes control measures, you can achieve stable glucose levels and improve your overall well-being. In this thorough guide, we will address many health challenges connected to sustaining long-term glucose health and present evidence-based options for sustainable and successful glucose management.

THE IMPORTANCE OF GLUCOSE HEALTH: Glucose health is crucial for everyone, regardless of whether they have diabetes or not. Stable glucose levels contribute to overall energy levels, cognitive function, and overall health. For patients with diabetes, maintaining normal glucose levels is particularly critical to prevent complications and improve quality of life.

ADOPTING A HEALTHY LIFESTYLE:

A healthy lifestyle forms the foundation for preserving long-term glycemic wellness. The following strategies can help you create sustainable lifestyle changes:

1. Balanced Diet: Emphasize a balanced and diverse diet that contains whole grains, lean meats, healthy fats, and plenty of fruits and vegetables. Limit processed foods, sugary beverages, and foods high in saturated and trans fats. Consult with a qualified dietitian to establish a personalized meal plan that satisfies your nutritional needs while regulating glucose levels efficiently.

2. frequent Physical Activity: Engage in frequent exercise or physical activity tailored to your fitness level and medical condition. Aim for a combination of aerobic exercise (such as brisk walking, swimming, or cycling) and strength training. Regular physical activity helps your body

utilize glucose more efficiently, improves insulin sensitivity, and aids weight management.

3. Weight regulation: Achieving and maintaining a healthy weight is vital for glucose regulation. If overweight or obese, work with a healthcare practitioner to design a specific weight loss strategy that includes a balanced diet, frequent physical exercise, and behavior change tactics.

4. Stress Management: Chronic stress might influence glucose levels. Practice stress management techniques such as deep breathing exercises, mindfulness meditation, yoga, or engaging in hobbies and activities you enjoy. Prioritize self-care and develop healthy strategies to cope with stress.

EFFICIENT GLUCOSE MONITORING: Regular monitoring of glucose levels is crucial for efficient glucose management. The following tips can help:

1. Blood Glucose Monitoring: If you have diabetes, regularly monitor your blood glucose levels using a glucometer or continuous glucose monitoring system. Follow your healthcare provider's recommendations for the frequency of tests and target ranges. Keep a log of your readings to spot patterns and share them with your healthcare provider during follow-up appointments.

2. A1C Testing: A1C testing shows an average of your blood glucose levels over the preceding two

to three months. It is an important tool for long-term glucose management. Discuss with your healthcare physician how often you should undergo A1C testing to assess your overall glucose management.

3. Use of Technology: Explore technological innovations like smartphone apps, wearable gadgets, and glucose monitoring systems that provide real-time data, reminders, and trends analysis. These tools can help you stay on track with your glucose management goals and provide vital insights.

MEDICATION MANAGEMENT: For persons with diabetes, medication management is typically important to maintain appropriate glucose levels.

The following measures can promote good medication management:

1. Adherence to Medications: Take your prescription medications as instructed by your healthcare practitioner. Follow the suggested dosages and schedules, and don't skip or vary them without consulting your healthcare team. Medication adherence has a critical role in obtaining and maintaining glycemic control.

2. Regular Follow-up: Schedule regular follow-up sessions with your endocrinologist or healthcare provider to monitor your glucose levels, discuss medication modifications if required, and address any concerns or issues you may have.

3. Education and Empowerment: Understand your medications, their mechanism of action, potential side effects, and interactions. Seek clarity from your healthcare practitioner or pharmacist to ensure you are well-informed about your prescription regimen.

EMOTIONAL SUPPORT AND SELF-CARE:
Maintaining long-term glucose health also involves attention to mental well-being and self-care:

1. Support System: Build a strong support system by enlisting family, friends, or support groups who understand and empathize with your struggle. Having a network of individuals who can

provide emotional support and encouragement can be enormously useful.

2. Diabetes Education: Attend diabetes education classes or workshops where you can learn more about managing your disease properly. These programs give practical solutions, suggestions, and counseling on glucose monitoring, food planning, and coping with the emotional elements of diabetes.

3. Self-Care Practices: Engage in self-care activities that enhance relaxation, emotional well-being, and overall health. Practice proper sleep hygiene, prioritize hobbies and activities that bring you joy, and set aside time for relaxation and stress reduction.

ENDS NOTE

Maintaining long-term glucose health needs dedication, persistence, and a holistic approach to lifestyle and glucose management. By adopting a healthy lifestyle, monitoring glucose levels regularly, properly managing medications, and emphasizing emotional well-being, you can achieve sustained glucose control and enhance your overall health and quality of life. Remember to communicate with your healthcare team for individualized guidance and assistance targeted to your specific requirements. By applying these evidence-based measures, you can take charge of your glucose health and boost your well-being in the long run.

Made in United States
Troutdale, OR
06/21/2024